# The Power of Mindsets

Jeremy Lopez

# POWER OF MINDSETS

By Dr. Jeremy Lopez

Copyright © 2014 by Jeremy Lopez

All rights reserved. This book is protected under the copyright laws of the United States of America. This book may not be copied or reprinted for commercial gain or profit. The use of short quotations or occasional page copying for personal or group study is permitted and encouraged.

Published by Identity Network

P.O. Box 383213

Birmingham, AL 35238

www.identitynetwork.net

United States of America

The author can be contacted at customerservice@identitynetwork.net

Book design by
Treasure Image & Publishing
TreasureImagePublishing.com
248.403.8046

# The Power of Mindsets

Jeremy Lopez

# TABLE OF CONTENTS

The Power of Mindsets ........................................................... 7

Thoughts Become Things! ...................................................... 9

Energy Is In The House! ........................................................ 11

Everything Is Made Up Of Energy ......................................... 13

Everything is Vibration, Frequency, and Waves ..................... 15

Wholeness and Unlimitedness Is God's Substance ................. 19

Mindsets Can Be Shifted Within A Second! ........................... 21

Tower of Babel ...................................................................... 25

Time to Wake Up! ................................................................. 29

I Attracted a New iPad! ......................................................... 37

Timing of the Delivery Is Not Your Concern ......................... 39

Don't Let That Thought Harden! ........................................... 41

Listen to Your Surroundings, It's Prophesying to You! .......... 43

Never Say Never .................................................................... 45

Do You Have a Vision For The Use of These Things? ........... 49

And The Winner Is… ............................................................. 51

What Does Zoe Mean Again? ................................................ 53

Movie Time ........................................................................... 57

Change Your View and the Way You Think of Yourself ........ 63

Create Your Reality ............................................................... 69

What Does Awareness Mean? ............................................... 71

You Are Called To Be the Observer of Your Own Thoughts ................. 73

Money and How to Think About It .......................................................... 77

God Gives the Increase, But Not the Money ............................................ 79

Check Out These Folks ................................................................................ 81

Biography ...................................................................................................... 85

Other Titles by Dr. Lopez ............................................................................ 89

# The Power of Mindsets

Let's take a look at mindsets and figure out how we are called to change them.

<u>Mindsets are very powerful.</u> Mindsets can be established when we are a child; or even when we get into our teenage years. Everyone on planet earth have mindsets within them that have been developed by their own belief system. Beliefs are extremely powerful! Mindsets grow as we begin to feed into them and give them our attention. I don't think people pay attention or understand that we have so much power in us from God. We have the potential to feed into anything that passes through our brain and make it expand and grow within us to become substance in our reality that can alter our entire life. Anything that is presented to your mind in thought form, you have the power to charge it up positively or negatively; the choice has been left up

to you. So as we look at mindsets, we need to remember that mindsets are established here on Earth, but yet created through the soulish realm to explode into the reality of this natural world.

# *Thoughts Become Things!*

Everything you think, and give your attention to, becomes a part of your life sooner or later. Throughout your life you will find yourself giving into idols, which are mindsets that have been established by the power of your attention with an intention. Intention within a mindset feeds it, empowers it and gives it exactly what it needs to bring forth definition, instruction and purpose.

A mindset sets itself into motion through YOUR life-giving attention. Thoughts become things that start in 'thought form' and manifest into 'substance form' when it is released from its cocoon. The cocoon comes from the metamorphosis process of the mind that takes every thought (that you give attention to), and causes it to grow from a small thought (caterpillar form) into a mindset (the butterfly form). Remember, thoughts grow!

They grow into mindsets when you feed into them. Anything you feed grows! Mindsets draw to us physical realities that reflect what we are thinking.

## We Behold What We Think

If we think negative thoughts about negative people, we are going to attract negative people and circumstances. If we think positive thoughts then we become magnets for positive people and positive situations.

# *Energy Is In The House!*

Do you realize that, as a magnet, you have the potential and the power to draw whatever it is you need into your life? Even scientists have determined that everything in the universe is made up of frequencies and vibrations. We need to remember that everything in the universe is light and energy slowed down into matter. Everything that is matter, if you speed it up, will return back to its original form; which is energy and light. We are matter that has been slowed down. If you speed us up again, we will become energy and light.

Matthew 5:14- *"Ye are the light of the world. A city that is set on an hill cannot be hid."*

Always remember, light is nature's way of transferring energy through space. We could make it complicated by talking about the mixture of electric and magnetic fields, quantum mechanics, and all of that, but we always need to remember the basics of this truth--*light is energy.*

You have positive energy and negative energy. Have you ever been around a person that is always negative and constantly complaining? They do not radiate light, joy and the glory of God upon their lives. If you hang around that person long enough, you will be affected by their negativity because they are giving off negative energy. Don't forget, what you hang out with, you become! A lot of times we look at energy, light, vibrations and frequencies and think that it sounds a lot like new age. But we need to remember that Jesus spoke of light many times.

The Greek word for energy is *'Energeia.'* One of the meanings for the word, *'Energy,'* is, "*Activity and operation.*" Energy is not a religion. It has no persuasion toward right wing or left wing political view. Energy is not Atheist, Christian, Catholic or Buddhist.

# *Everything Is Made Up Of Energy*

According to Wikipedia, the definition for energy is: "a scalar physical quantity, an attribute of objects and systems that is conserved in nature (or the universe). In physics textbooks energy is often defined as the ability to do work or to generate heat."

When you are around people who are positive you begin to feel good and feel that positive energy. When you are in the presence of someone who is laughing and joyful, and has a positive glow about them, it tends to rub off on you, does it not? When people are negative and down, you will receive that negative energy which will lower your frequency.

# *Everything is Vibration, Frequency, and Waves*

Frequency is the measurable rate of electrical energy flow that is constant between any two points. Everything has frequency.

Going down to an atom, we know that, depending on the element, it has a particular frequency or vibration. Number of Atoms connected in particular structure creates molecules. How densely packed are these molecules that create the mass; like air, our body, or like a table and chair.

All of these vibrate at fixed frequencies.

Let's get to the basics of how our mind works and operates. All physical reality is made up of vibrations of energy. Your thoughts too are vibrations of energy. This is not some crazy theory, but rather the reality that quantum physics show us. Your thoughts have a powerful influence; they affect what happens to you. To know this is to know something great.

Therefore, when someone is not feeling good and they are down or depressed, it means they have a low frequency. Therefore we have to charge them up in their most holy faith.

Jude 20- *"But ye, beloved, building (charging) yourselves in your most holy faith."*

We are called to energize ourselves and those around us, build them up, and charge them up with unspeakable joy. If the Greek word for energy means, *"activity and operation,"* then we need to set forth a new mindset of health and wholeness into ourselves, and in those around us, by getting them 'active' in consciousness by shifting and altering them to think about something else, and cause that new thought to be set into 'operation' in their life. When we begin to make the shift in consciousness, we then see the vibrations increase toward *"hope and a bright future."*

Jeremiah 29:11- *"For I know the plans I have for you, declares the LORD, plans for welfare and not for evil, to give you a future and a hope."*

When someone is down and depressed they have a low frequency. We need to be able to charge them up by 'being' or 'becoming' our own thought of joy, happiness and hope. Our success literally depends on the quality and intensity of our thoughts. We need to take stock in our thoughts of success that carry with it an overflow; not just for ourselves but for others as well. If we are not careful, we may be operating with outdated and limited ideas, habits, attitudes, values, and beliefs. These old mental patterns keep us stuck in lack and limitation. We must replace all the old negative thoughts that have been 'programming' us and controlling us to do things that the real authentic self is not called to do. You have the capability to transform, *'by the renewing of your mind'*, everything that is negative in your thinking into something of substance that is positive.

Romans 12:2- *"And be not conformed to this world: but be ye transformed by the renewing of your mind, that ye may prove what is that good, and acceptable, and perfect, will of God."*

# *Wholeness and Unlimitedness Is God's Substance*

The transformation of your thoughts and mind will show you how to release those old mental patterns and take you where you want to go by formulating new habits and patterns that are unlimited for you. 'Unlimited' is where the Spirit mind in you sees everything; not just possible, but already accomplished and finished with integrity and excellence. Negative thoughts can never truly finish anything, accomplish anything or achieve anything. It can only give you the façade, or mask, that the negative thought has 'done it's job'; yet it is only a shadow, not the real thing. Wholeness and completion can only come from God; who is the author of 'good things.' Wholeness can only come out of the mind of God, which releases good things, completion, unlimitedness and overflowing.

# *Mindsets Can Be Shifted Within A Second!*

You have the power in you to shift from those old mental patterns instantly. Have you ever been around someone and thought to yourself how "old school" they are? You may get frustrated with them because they never want to progress in life. They have a 'dinosaur mentality' when it deals with new technology and computers. Since they are scared and fearful of new technology they tend to stay away from it. That is what fear does.

II Timothy 1:7- *"For God hath not given us the spirit of fear; but of power, and of love, and of a sound mind."*

Fear will take you down the wrong path and leave you in the room of 'non-productivity.' Fear keeps you paralyzed, trapped and left with 'no movement.' When you allow the fear of something you do not understand to create a new 'grid' within you, it begins to set up a mindset that says, "Stay away from it,' 'danger,' 'red flag,' 'it's not good for you,' 'it's harmful,' or 'it's bad". When you set up something in your mind to say, "*it scares me,*" then all of a sudden you mark it off as being wrong, bad, or dangerous. Anytime you stay in your mindset of comfort of what you "know", or what you're use to, the grid of your life never changes. It is time to change the grid of your life folks and start seeing things in a 'new light.'

**Light-** *"the form of energy that makes it possible to see things. Something that makes vision possible."*

You have to realize that old mindsets need to come down. The "old school" mentality that we have been taught all of our lives must come down. Let's take a look at how the consciousness of humanity has changed in the past 50 years, by looking at slavery. It took Martin Luther King Jr. years to change people's mindsets from saying, *"I'm not a second-class citizen. I don't have to be treated this way,"* to say, *"I know that I am somebody in God. I know that I can accomplish anything I put my hand to"*. For years, black people were convinced they were second-class citizens because of the mindset white people spread around. These mindsets came from the white community during that day, and their thoughts became their reality. A stronghold was created in the atmosphere during that time period through the common thinking of those who had been deceived that slavery was the correct and right thing to do. The more people you have to believe something (right or wrong), it will begin to create in the atmosphere a new belief or stronghold that will keep people bound to that belief until someone begins to be creative and speak *'Let there be...'* into the atmosphere.

Genesis 1:3- *"And God said, Let there be light: and there was light."*

*'Let there be,'* is the Genesis affect set into motion to open the heavens for a new way of living and thinking. It will begin to create a new grid in which others will consider and hopefully 'walk on the water' into the unknown territory by faith.

# *Tower of Babel*

Look in Genesis at the tower of Babel. These people had created in the atmosphere a mindset that they could reach God through the building of a tower. Everyone came together (law of attraction- like attracts like), through the magnetism of their conscious thoughts of reaching God.

Genesis 11:1-6 *"And the whole earth was of one language, and of one speech. And it came to pass, as they journeyed from the east, that they found a plain in the land of Shinar; and they dwelt there. And they said one to another, Go to, let us make brick, and burn them thoroughly. And they had brick for stone, and slime had they for morter. And they said, Go to, let us build us a city and a tower, whose top may reach unto heaven; and let us make us a name, lest we be scattered abroad upon the face of the whole earth. And the Lord came down to see the city and the tower, which the children of men built. And the Lord said, Behold, the people is one, and they have all one language; and this they begin to do: and now nothing will be restrained from them, which they have imagined to do."*

What they "thought" and "imagined" was happening. Mindsets find other similar mindsets and stick together. Law of attraction says, *"like attracts like."* You will build a stronghold with others who think like you. It's a fact. Your mindset needs others, like itself, with which to bond and reinforce itself.

People began to arise like Martin Luther King Jr. and proclaim freedom, liberty and equality for all. The more you hear something in your spirit and "listen" to it, your thoughts begin to shift; and a paradigm shift takes place. It always starts within one person. The mindset that you have previously set up in your life will begin to starve itself to death, since you have shifted from feeding it life, with your attention, to now feeding the 'new thought' with your attention and energy.

## Time to Wake Up!

When you begin to shift and change your mindset, you begin to awaken. Everyone on planet Earth will have some type of an awakening in his or her life. Many people will awaken through hearing or seeing principles, quotes, conversation pieces or by just having a revelation. Every thought that comes into your mind, carries with it an awakening to altar you. An 'awakening' will cause you to reexamine yourself, your job, your family and everything about you.

**Awakening-** *"the state of being conscious."*

**Awakening** means:

1. Rousing; quickening.
2. The act of awaking from sleep.
3. A revival of interest or attention.

4. A recognition, realization, or coming into awareness of something.
5. A renewal of interest in religion, especially in a community, a revival.

Old mindsets can destroy you, so you have to begin to make the paradigm shift in order to allow new healthy thoughts to arise in your mind. Therefore, when you look at yourself in the mirror, your perception of yourself will change and you see a brand new person. A paradigm is the sum total of our beliefs, values, ideas, expectations, attitudes, habits, decisions, opinions and thought patterns about ourselves and others. It is literally the filter through which we interpret what we see and what we experience.

**Paradigm-** *"a distinct concept or thought pattern" or "a typical example or pattern of something; a pattern or model."*

A mindset actually reshapes our life and it begins to reveal to you yourself as a direct reflection of it. You have to get it in your spirit to say, *"What I believe will happen because thoughts are powerful magnets. I have tested and judged what enters my mind and found it to be true or false.*" If I begin to believe that I can accomplish something and begin to believe that nothing is impossible for me in life to achieve, than I can do whatever I has set before me to do. I can do anything God has willed for me to do because God has empowered me with His DNA and also His creative, powerful mind. All I have to do is think it, act upon it and then I will have it. When I begin to believe that, my thoughts begin to be energized because they begin to find something to shape or reshape in this world.

**DNA-** "**Deoxyribonucleic acid** *(DNA) is a molecule that encodes the genetic instructions used in the development and functioning of all known living organisms and many viruses. DNA is a nucleic acid; alongside proteins and carbohydrates, nucleic acids compose the three major macromolecules essential for all known forms of life.*"

We have God's DNA inside of us to think and then act out that thought; to manifest it in our reality so we can either enjoy it or learn from it. The thoughts that we think will draw into our lives (by the same frequency wave of that thought) exactly what we desire from within the heart. It will become a manifestation in our reality sooner than we think. We need to always keep in mind, that our brain has been created by God to be powerful, magnetic, creative and imaginative.

**Magnet–** *"is an object made from a material that is magnetized and creates its own persistent magnetic field."*

The magnet that once drew the negativity in my life, will now begin to draw to me the positive things I need; and all I had to do was to "think." Anything in life that I need, as I begin to think positive, God will begin to orchestrate creation, and the universe, to bring to me what I desire from His will; and even bring people of precious like-faith to back me up in my endeavor.

If I have a thought that formulates into a mindset of defeat, then I will begin to draw people that will rip me off, tear me down and take advantage of me; because my mindset prophesied to me that I am a defeated person and I believed it. When I begin to change my mindset to say, *"I believe I am a victor. I believe I am more than a conqueror. I believe I can achieve and accomplish anything I want to do because I am a champion"*. It's not necessarily what you say, but what you think. True, powerful thoughts come from the heart. The Bible says, *"As a man thinketh in his heart"*.

Proverbs 23:7- *"For as he thinketh in his heart, so is he: Eat and drink, saith he to thee; but his heart is not with thee."*

> ***"Your life is governed by what you think. Your thoughts are the steering wheel of your life. If the waters of your life look rough and you see the boat headed into the storm, just change the way you're thinking and the boat of your life will shift 180 degrees to calmer waters." - Jeremy Lopez***

The thoughts you think in your heart are extremely powerful, and you will begin to draw those same people like a magnet who are champions, winners, entrepreneurs, and victors.

**Law of Attraction-** *"is the universal law that "like attracts like" and that by focusing on positive or negative thoughts, one can bring about positive or negative results. The law of attraction says that people and their thoughts are both made from "pure energy", and the belief that like energy attracts like energy."*

God will draw the right people to you in your *"network"* or *"vibrational wave"* that will begin to build a healthy relationship with you. They will begin to feed into that thought because they are in the same *"frequency wave"* of joy, laughter, strength, victory and overcoming. They will begin to be drawn to you, as you will begin to be drawn to them, because of the "precious like-faith" (magnetism) mentality.

John 12:32- *"And I, if I be lifted up from the earth, will draw all men unto me."*

Where is Christ? He is in His people. Where are people going to be drawn? To the Christ in you! Get ready, people are going to be drawn to you according to "how" you live your life, and "what" you're thinking about your life.

Let me give you an example of shifting the mind and how thoughts begin to change your lifestyle.

# I Attracted a New iPad!

A friend of mine, which is actually one of our employees, desired an iPad; and he thought about it for a long time. He knew the law of attraction, he understood the principles of the Kingdom and he knew the bible said, *"As a man thinketh in his heart, so is he."*

He knew the desires of his heart was that God wanted him to have good technology, that he could rely on, because he knew that the internet would produce money for him. You see, he already had a vision for why he wanted an iPad. So he began to ponder and think about what kind he wanted. He was creating what he desired for his life. A couple of months later, I was on my speaking tour. He went with me to assist with my books and teaching CDs. As we were on the tour, he was assisting some people one night with my new book. All of the sudden, a young lady began to express the love she has for my teachings and books. In her hand was a brand new iPad that she felt led to buy for him. She just knew in her heart that it was something that she needed to buy, and 'who' was going to receive it. That's how precise and defined your thoughts need to be, to bring into your life exactly what you want for your destiny. It is so important for you to know the details of what you want, and how it will look. We need to remember that people can be used by God to deliver what "you're desiring." This woman walked right up to him and said, *"Here you go. God led me to purchase this iPad for you."* His face illuminated from the place of expectancy and thankfulness, but it also came from a place in his heart where his creative ability said, **'Let there be.......an iPad.'** He knew that thoughts become things. He pondered upon it, not knowing the time frame, but he believed it would happen in God's timing.

# *Timing of the Delivery Is Not Your Concern*

Understand the time frame is not your business. The perfect time of the Kingdom of God will bring it 'fresh and hot' from the Heavens to you.

When you begin to be positive and focus on the good things, they begin to happen to you. But it could take days, weeks, months, or even years. God knows when you need it and it is always in His perfect timing. He knows everything about your life and He knows when you need to be presented with the idea, or the manifestation, of that thought. For my friend it was not that long, only a couple of months, and actually he began to see it already on it's way to him. Are you hungry enough to start seeing the glass half full instead of half empty? When we begin to see things through

His eyes, we will find the good and the positive in everything He created. So, we have the power in our mind to pull into our lives what we need; for the good of who we are in Him, and also for the good of others around us.

# *Don't Let That Thought Harden!*

You might ask, *"How does all of this deal with mindsets?"* Easy. Your life has been what it 'has been' simply because the stronghold in your mind has kept you walking the plank of the ship long enough; until you jumped off and realized how miserable you have been. Mindsets are formed just like concrete. When the granular material is added to water to make the concrete, it starts off as a thick, yet fluid, element. As time goes by, it becomes so hard that it would hold hundreds upon hundreds of pounds and not even think about cracking. Mindsets are formed the same way. Once you give attention to a thought, your attention gives it what it needs to create the process of hardening. Once hardened, by your attention and energy, it sets itself up as a stronghold, an idol or the most common terminology used today, a mindset. We will find ourselves 'bowing' to that idol every second of the day until some other thought greater enters into our lives that we find more satisfying.

**Concrete-** *"is a composite material composed of water, coarse granular material (the fine and coarse aggregate or filler) embedded in a hard matrix of material (the cement or binder) that fills the space among the aggregate particles and glues them together."*

Are you bowing to the "me" syndrome in your mind? Or are you bowing to the image of Christ by decreasing, so that image of God can increase in your mind and become a healthy mindset of victory.

# *Listen to Your Surroundings, It's Prophesying to You!*

The universe is going to set in motion the thoughts that you have given life. God uses creation, and the universe, to help bring things in our path so we can see the 'detour' sign and hopefully follow it to a better way of thinking and living.

God uses creation to get you where you need to be. You have creation trying to help you change your thoughts as well! God is setting you up to reexamine your thoughts. Someone, and something, is prophesying to you….are you listening?

**Romans 8:19-23** - *For the earnest expectation of the creature waiteth for the manifestation of the sons of*

*God. For the creature was made subject to vanity, not willingly, but by reason of him who hath subjected the same in hope, Because the creature itself also shall be delivered from the bondage of corruption into the glorious liberty of the children of God. For we know that the whole creation groaneth and travaileth in pain together until now.*

Creation is being set free as we move towards our destiny and align ourselves where we need to be. Creation wants to be set free from the damage caused by Adam. So God uses creation to put things in our path so we can see it, ponder it, then create it in our consciousness. Once we think it, it becomes reality and it gets creation closer to the freedom God intended.

# Never Say Never

So, let's say you're constantly pondering on the thought of, *"I will never get sick."* or *"I will never be poor,"* you have to stop and realize that what the universal, kingdom law of attraction focuses on is the actual noun, or main word, you're saying. This is the way God has orchestrated it; by the law of attraction. What the focus becomes is not the fact that you don't want it, but the fact that you are still bringing forth the negative word; or the word you are trying to get rid of in your life! The fact that you don't want it does not mean you will not get it. You are still meditating and giving attention to what you don't want, instead of focusing on what you do want! Instead of saying, *"I don't want to be poor anymore,"* say, *"I'm so glad I have such an amazing amount of abundance."* If not, the law of attraction is going to focus on the word, "sick."

Don't say, *"I don't want to be <u>sick</u>"* or 'I don't want to be <u>poor</u>." Because your focus is still on the negative side of it. Also, If you say, *"One day I'm going to have money"*, you are focusing on the money aspect, but you are also throwing it to the future.

Philippians 4:6- "*.....let your requests be <u>made known</u> unto God.*"

What you are requesting are the <u>details</u> of what you want! Remember, God says, *"I call those things that be not, as though it were"*. God speaks present tense, which means when I begin to focus on things that I need and want in my life, I begin to place myself in the now moment; as if I own it already.

Romans 4:17- *"As it is written, I have made you a father of many nations in the presence of Him whom He believed-God, who gives life to the dead, and calls those things which do not exist as though they did."*

We need to begin to declare, *"I am whole now,"* *"I feel wonderful now,"* and *"I am joyful now."* I begin to focus

NOT on some futuristic thing down the road, but on what I already have now.

II Corinthians 6:2- "......*behold, now is the accepted time; behold, now is the day of salvation.*"

I just need to awaken to know that everything that I will ever need for my future is already inside of me. I just need to awaken to it!

Romans 13:11- "*And that, knowing the time, that* **now it is high time to awake out of sleep.**"

"*I'm going to be happy.*" "*One day this is going to happen for me.*" "*One day I'm going to have a business.*" Once I change from a "one day" mentality, I will begin to bring the future into my now. When you desire a house, car or anything nice in your life and you begin to say to yourself, "*One day I am going to have that,*" it will be pushed back on a day in the future that will never come true. You have got to begin to place yourself like God and live in the now moment, it's the eternal I AMNESS of who God is. You have to place yourself in that "now" thought and then BE (or awaken) that reality of the thought inside of you. See yourself driving that car now. Visualize your hand wrapped around that steering wheel, driving that new car. See a key in your hand turning to unlock the door of your new home. When you begin to focus and put yourself in that car, or that home, you begin to get the feeling of how good it feels, smells, and looks to be in that car or home. You begin to bring it to the now and it begins to happen quicker for you. It begins to come to you quicker because your thoughts begin to accelerate your emotions of joy, happiness, and peace.

# Do You Have a Vision For The Use of These Things?

Do you want a very important key? It's not all about the big things, or how you see it, it's about *"what are you going to do with it once you get it"*? Therefore, you have to get a vision on what you will do with the car and how it will benefit you, others and God. You have to offer up a definition to God to say why you need it.

Proverbs 29:18- *"Where there is no vision, the people perish."*

God does not give money to the ignorant. You must have a vision for everything you create and desire in your life. If I asked you, *"Do you need money?"* and you say, *"Absolutely, I need money,"* and then I ask you,

"*What are you going to do with the money?*" If you can't come up with a quick answer because you have no vision or destiny for that substance you are wanting, you really don't need it! This is when it just becomes materialistic. Remember, "*Without a vision, the people (or things) perish.*" In other words, anything that has not been fed a vision will not last and will perish.

# *And The Winner Is...*

Statistics say that around 90% of people who have won the lottery, have lost it very quick. This happens simply because their poverty mindset keeps them from prospering. Unless you have rich, healthy thoughts to know how to handle money, and great wealth, you will not be able to handle it in the natural. You can only prosper in the natural when you have mastered the art of building a healthy mindset of understanding how to handle, spend, invest and expand wealth. Statistics go on to say the reason the 90% of people who won the lottery end up losing all the money they won is because they do not know how to manage it. Their thought patterns are still in an old mindset and they never knew what it was like to prosper in their mind first, before God prospered them in the natural. You have to change your *"stinking thinking,"* and move on up to something bigger; something bigger than you.

Hosea 4:6- *"My people are destroyed for lack of knowledge."*

You have to begin to prosper your mind in order to know how to handle the vision, how to handle the money, how to handle the car or how to handle the home. You must begin to learn how to handle things in your life that you are desiring that God has no problem with you having. You will need to realign yourself so that God is the head of your life, not the thing you seek. Once He is the head of your life, and you are operating in His mind, you have every right to begin to think, focus and ponder on the God thoughts in you to have the Zoe kind of life you desire.

# *What Does Zoe Mean Again?*

Zoe means the, "God kind of life."

John 5:26- "For as the Father has life (zoe) in Himself, so He has granted the Son to have life (zoe) in Himself."

The Greek word translated "life" in our text today is "Zoe."

God has no problem with you having anything in this life because He wants you to accelerate. He wants you to be wealthy in every area of your life. But you have to begin to set your mind on things above and not on things of this world. What does that mean?

Colossians 3;2- "Set your mind (and thoughts) on things above and not on the things of this world."

There is a principle and a protocol in the Kingdom of God that means you first have to set your mind and thoughts on things above; which is God. You must first focus on God to figure out what He wants for your life. God's thoughts are unlimited, boundless and overflowing. He wants you to prosper and be in good health EVEN AS YOUR SOUL PROSPERS. The soul is the mind, will and emotions. The mind is your thoughts!

III John 1:2- "Beloved, I wish above all things that thou mayest prosper and be in health, even as thy soul prospereth."

I want to reiterate that God has no problem whatsoever with you having the finer things in life. But, you have got to make sure He is #1 by seeking the Kingdom of God first, and then God will bless you with the things.

Matthew 6:33- "But seek ye first the kingdom of God, and his righteousness; and all these things shall be added unto you."

So as you begin to put Him first in your life, and set your thoughts on things above, it will bring your thinking to a higher consciousness. It begins to renew your mind where you can learn how to handle the big things of life. It's time to train your mind to handle "big things" in thought form. So your mind must prosper with new mindsets in order to go higher.

## Movie Time

Let's say you rent a movie and start watching it on your television. As you get halfway through it, you realize how boring and bad this movie really is. What do you do? You remove the movie from your DVD player and put something else in to watch. In this analogy, your mind is the television and the movie is your thoughts. We need to understand if we do not like what we see, change the situation or the station. Let's say you are visualizing your own life. Is your life and thought process fun, energetic, exciting, clean, wholesome, joyful, full of laughter that everyone from all ages can watch? Or is your mind rated R? Maybe it's very boring and needs some adventure added to it? You hold the remote in your hand, and in your mind, to just change what you are watching. If there is something you don't like on television, you don't beat your television up, you just change the station. Change your visuals and it will change what you are seeing on the screen.

It is time to make the shift on the movie screen of our mind, and begin to visualize what it is you want to see. You don't destroy the television, you get rid of the movie. It's the same principle with your mind. If you watched the movie of your thoughts, would you be completely satisfied or would you be disgusted at the non-productivity? How many of you have ever watched a movie and said, *"I don't like what I'm watching. It's depressing and sad"*. What do you do about it? You make a healthy change by either walking out of the theater or pulling the movie out of the DVD player.

When someone else sees the reality of your life, what they are really seeing are the thoughts that were once in seed form, and are now full grown manifesting into the reality of your life.

Remember, your thoughts do become things. People will see how easy it is to read someone's thoughts because our thoughts become actions in this natural world and actions speak louder than any words.

Have you ever been around a person that has been fired from 7 or 8 jobs and you find them blaming those jobs for treating them bad and taking advantage of them? But in reality, if you are on the outside of the situation observing that person, you would see, most of the time, the problem is not with the jobs but with the person. That person ends up being deceived by themselves because of the mindsets they have built up within them to believe everyone is out to get them. Deception keeps the wall around the mindset you have created to help protect it from the truth that could set it free.

The mindset of that person convinced them that their boss, or manager, was taking advantage of them. Therefore, they have been deceived by the illusion of their own thoughts; because they never learned to monitor their thoughts. They never learned to be the observer of their own mind and see how it looks and sounds from an outside point of view. The mindset they should have from God should say, *"I have examined my life, and I have done something wrong here. I have discovered that I messed up on my job. The best thing for me to do is to learn from my mistake and go on".* So they can begin to change their life and set forth a healthier pattern of living for themselves.

The word 'repentance' means to *"change your mind or you're thinking around."* Greek word for 'repentance' is **"metanoeó."**

It means, *"To, change my mind (or thoughts), change the inner man."*

We need to find ourselves repenting and turning our "thinking" around, and start realizing that the problem may be within us. Instead of blaming or coming down on yourself, just make the paradigm shift to say, *'I will never think that way or do it that way again.'* Begin to think good thoughts of working with wonderful and sweet people. But you must see yourself as wonderful, sweet, kind, loving, long suffering, having patience and caring before you attract those wonderful people. It must first begin inwardly before it will manifest outwardly. Therefore, you have to monitor your thoughts and look at them and say, *"I've got to change the way I've been thinking"*. You have to change your mindset and recognize that subconsciously you have been letting out mean and negative thoughts towards others for a while now. You need to begin to change your mindset, and then realize you need to think good things and good thoughts. See yourself as a happy and joyful person that loves people. Monitor your thoughts and give life to only good wholesome thoughts. Before you know it, you will be on a job where people will love you and you will get promotions and raises. Learn to train, and convince, your mind that you work with a great team of people. We must recognize our character depends on us respecting ourselves enough to start caring for what enters into our mind and body.

# Change Your View and the Way You Think of Yourself

It's time to deal with the low self-esteem issues in our lives. A lot of times, these issues of low self-esteem come up in areas of jobs, family and relationships. Low self-esteem always looks at everyone else and says, "They just don't understand me."

Let's also examine the way we see our job. If you have the attitude that you are not the problem on your job, that it is everyone else, we need to take a deeper look at ourselves. We need to have a wake up call to change our thoughts in order to birth forth a healthier way we see ourselves and others. It might be you're worshipping the idol, or mindset, you have created in your subconscious mind that does not allow you to see what is on the other side of it; which is a different outlook on life and people. This gives you an expanded look of how things really are in your life that you don't see about yourself.

If you were a "fly on the wall" viewing yourself, you would probably see yourself as a slacker, showing up late and leaving early, and doing things only half way and never giving that company 100% of your time. You might see yourself doing just enough to "barely get by" on that job. It could be we have deceived ourselves in believing the paradigm in our mind, that we have created somewhere in our lives, a mentality that people are out to get us.

Galatians 6:3- *"For if a man **think** himself to be something, when he is nothing, he deceiveth himself."*

Notice Genesis 6:3 talks about if a man THINKS himself to be something. Did you know you have that powerful to even, *"think yourself to be something."*

What do you think yourself to be? In order to make this scripture powerful for you *"to create yourself to be something,"* you must "think yourself" through the will of God, so you will fill the void of the "nothingness" that creeps up now and then. It's time to "think yourself" and then "know yourself" to become that thought of how God "thinks" about you.

Remember, the law of the kingdom in "thoughts becoming things," needs to be balanced on not just the "me" syndrome, but the "us" mentality. Life actually is about what you can do and give to other people. I can always tell when a person is truly thinking a 'God-thought' as opposed to a "me-thought" because they come into a place of an awakening in the Spirit and they think bigger beyond themselves. They start monitoring their thoughts and begin to think positively about the outcome including more than just them. They begin to feed into their spirit healthy and wonderful thoughts. As they hear 'God-thoughts,' they will begin to say, *"How can I help other people with what I am thinking through the mind of Christ; since*

*His thoughts in me expand beyond what I'm able to ask or think? What can I do to be a blessing? How can I do a better job serving others in my creative abilities?"* Thoughts become things, and if it's going to be a "God-thing" then it must be about others. In order for you to find advancement in your own life you need to advance the lives of other people. And that doesn't mean to sit quietly and do your job and do it right and not affect anyone else. It means you must go to the highest degree, go to the degree where you are incorporating others in your vision (visualization) to help empower them as you empower yourself and climb the corporate ladder of success. It's time you begin to have these "God-thoughts" and change your mindset. You begin to move in the God consciousness and ask what you can do for others. Even in the boundary of prophecy, we have edification, exhortation and comfort. So you need to move over into the law of sowing and reaping in order to receive the harvest that has been promised to you.

The law of sowing and reaping always incorporates others into whom you can sow. You begin to think good things about other people. God is always about giving. God is never about just receiving. If you are going to think "God-thoughts" in order to set into motion a new way of thinking, and looking at things in a different light, you need to move over in what God "lives in"; which is expansion and multiplication. Which means, you need to expand past just the "me" syndrome and get into a "universal" mindset so life becomes broader for you to be *all things to all people."*

*II Corinthians 9:2- "I am made all things to all men..."*

Because thoughts are powerful magnets and they draw to you exactly what you are thinking. The Bible says, *"according to your faith it shall be done to you"*, another word for faith is "belief."

Matthew 9:29- *"According to your faith be it unto you."*

# Create Your Reality

Whatever you're believing, that thought it's going to be done unto you. We need to start examining our mindsets and begin to question whether they support us, or limit us. Many of us have put our minds on "auto-pilot." Do not allow your mind to be set on auto-pilot. Because we need to monitor our thoughts throughout the day in order to stay fresh, new and inventive. Examine your thoughts and awaken to say, *"What do I want to create today?"*

Let's say you are in your car and you're going to a destination that is 200 miles away. So you put your car on cruise control, begin to listen to the radio and let the car drive itself. You still need to be looking ahead of you, watching for stop signs, red lights, and for turns; plus continuing to have your hand on the steering wheel at all times. When you go around a curve, you will still have to put your foot on the brake in order to slow down to make the turn. A car on cruise control does not mean it will drive you everywhere you need to go without you being a part of it; it only means it will control the flow of fuel for you. In comparison, with the thoughts in your mind, you will still need to walk in awareness, and be alert for what lies ahead of you. You will still have to steer, and remain in control, to get to your destination.

# *What Does Awareness Mean?*

**Awareness**- is the state or ability to perceive, to feel, or to be conscious of events, objects, or sensory patterns. In this level of consciousness, sense data can be confirmed by an observer without necessarily implying understanding. More broadly, it is the state or quality of being aware of something. In biological psychology, awareness is defined as a human's or an animal's perception and cognitive reaction to a condition or event.

Your mind should never be placed on auto-pilot. You should always stop and smell the coffee to make sure you like it or not. It's your choice, your call. Be aware of your present now reality, the now moment. The now moment is the place where you are truly alive and awake. When you stop, look and listen, it opens up the door for awareness. Pay attention, the now moment is calling out to you.

# You Are Called To Be the Observer of Your Own Thoughts

You need to stop and monitor your thoughts. Find yourself saying, "I should have stopped on that thought and paid attention to it," or "I should have dismissed that thought since it is not going to produce anything for me." You have to learn to monitor your thoughts. Let me give you an example concerning mindsets, thoughts, and even money.

> *"We create our own mindset but at some point our mindsets will begin to create us."*
> *– Jeremy Lopez*

There once was a young girl name Samantha. Samantha grew up in a place where her parents had money; and she always believed that money would come from her parents. When she was a small child, whether she wanted ice cream, dolls, or presents, she knew her parents had the money for it and would buy it for her. She knew that money would always be there for her from her parents no matter what. As she got older, she became a cheerleader because she knew her parents would supply the need for her uniform and all the things she would need to be the best cheerleader she could be. Throughout time, her parents provided for her a car, prom dress, books, gas money and all the essentials she would need to make the transition into adulthood. As she went out on her own, she discovered things were different for her now. She could not function in society, simply because she had a mindset that said, *"Money comes from my parents."* So even as she got older she was constantly borrowing money from her parents, because she was not taught to be self-sufficient.

As time went on, she never allowed her mind to grow with her life. She never taught herself to establish a new mindset that money does not come from her parents, but from what she could produce within herself. So the mindset she had was on "overtime." It served no purpose anymore like it once did for the younger self. Like Samantha, we must come to the place in our lives where we reexamine our mind to see if what we "believe", or have "set into concrete", is still serving us in this hour. If not, it will mess us up, keep us from destiny and draw things to us by the law of attraction that we no longer want to be a part of our lives. It begins to be clutter and not blessing.

# *Money and How to Think About It*

Money does not come from the bank. Money is first of all employed by your thoughts. Your thought of money has to expand into a belief in order for it to materialize. Money comes as a result of your thoughts. Money is a spiritual thing, it is not a natural thing. Your mindset produces money. Think about how Donald Trump must think when he deals with buying and selling businesses, stock market trades, who to "hire and fire" and making investments. He's either standing by what he knows and feels comfort in, or he is constantly expanding and challenging his mindsets to shift and grow in new ideas and create new atmospheres. He realizes money doesn't come from his parents, the bank or any building he owns; money is a result of his thoughts. His thoughts must constantly create new forms of life, so he can see them materialize into what he wants and needs for his life.

# God Gives the Increase, But Not the Money

Nowhere in the Bible does it say that God gives us money.

Proverbs 13:22- *"the wealth of the sinner is <u>laid up</u> for the just."*

Deuteronomy 8:18- *"You shall remember the LORD your God, for it is He who gives you power <u>to get</u> wealth."*

I Corinthians 3:7- *"So neither the one who plants nor the one who waters is anything, but only God, <u>who makes</u> things increase."*

If you notice in the scriptures above, they use the words, *"laid up," "to get"* and *"who makes."* You must learn to expand your consciousness and be creative, through the mind of Christ, "who makes" (I Cor. 3:7) increase spring up in you to "get" (Deut. 8:18) what is "laid up" (Prov. 13:32) for you to posses. How can you multiply that money? Through the power of your mind! You have to learn how to employ your thoughts, and make them work for you.

II Thessalonians 3:10- *"If anyone is not willing to work, then he is not to eat, either."*

You have to work in order to get what you want to eat in your life. Learn to work your mind, not your behind. Then put your thoughts to work for you. Good healthy thoughts produce good things in your life. Our mindsets drive our life in every area. If you're poor, remove the driver called "poverty" and replace it with a new driver called "wealth".

# Check Out These Folks

If you want to get a good look at how you think, and how those around you think, try playing a game of cards with them. Take a look at those around you as they make a play. All of a sudden, their mood begins to change. Everything about them begins to shift. The plays people do around the card table usually speak of what, and how, they live their lives in different situations. Do some people seem like they are bored with the game? Do others become automatically competitive? Do some tend to be easy going through the game? Do some act real cool with a good "poker face"? Do some alienate other players in order to control and dominate? Sometimes in card games people tend to turn into monsters. Some begin to become isolated, look out for themselves, defensive, or become competitive. Some people become afraid they will be taken advantage of or made to look silly throughout the game. All of these "behaviors" reflect certain mindsets. This is a way of looking at oneself, others, and the world around you. When people play cards, they tend to act out their thoughts of how they view themselves and others. Their mindsets tend to "take them over" and be in control. People begin to change into "another person." You need to examine the "other person" that you have become since it is your mindset acting out through you. If you become the observer of yourself, you will either like how you're acting or you will change that "other" person immediately. These are traits of how you really think about yourself. You have to learn how to monitor your thoughts and take control of them. Begin to set up a new mindset in your life where you become the one who is in charge of YOU and not the mindset. Because you (the observer) know the goals you want to accomplish. A mindset cannot create; it just obeys and expands out of what it is. YOU are the co-creator! YOU are the observer in charge!

It is time to bring the joy into your world. It is time for you to get the job you want in your life. It is your time NOW to think, believe and manifest what you want. Change your thoughts and you will change your world….guaranteed.

# *Biography*

Dr. Jeremy Lopez is the Founder and President of Identity Network International and Now is Your Moment. Identity Network is a prophetic resource website that reaches well over 153,000 people around the globe and distributes books and teaching CD's. Jeremy has taught and prophesied to thousands of people from all walks of life such as local church congregations, producers, investors, business owners, attorneys, city leaders, musicians, and various ministries around the world concerning areas such as finding missing children, financial breakthroughs, parenthood, and life changing decisions.

Dr. Jeremy Lopez is an international teacher and motivational speaker. Dr. Jeremy speaks on new dimensions of revelatory knowledge in scripture, universal laws, mysteries, patterns, and cycles. He has a love for all people and desires to enrich their lives with love, grace and the mercy of God and to empower them to be successful. Dr. Jeremy believes it is time to awake the Christ Conscious mind and live out the victorious life that was meant for us. His desire is to live a life filled with purpose, potential, and destiny. He ministers with such prophetic revelation that brings a freshness of the word of the Lord to people everywhere.

This is accomplished through conferences, prophetic meetings, and seminars. He serves on many governing boards, speaks to business leaders across the nation, and also holds a Doctorate of Divinity. He has had the privilege of ministering prophetically to Governor Bob Riley of Alabama. He has also ministered to thousands overseas including millionaires around the world. He has traveled to many nations including Jamaica, Prague, Paris, Indonesia, Haiti, Hong Kong, Taiwan, UK, Mexico, Singapore, Bahamas, Costa Rica, Puerto

Rico, etc. He has hosted and been a guest on several radio and TV programs from Indonesia to New York.

He is the author of nationally published books, 'Abandoned to Divine Destiny,' 'The Power of the Eternal Now'(Destiny Image) and his newest book, 'Releasing the Power of the Prophetic'(Chosen Books). He has also recorded over 45 teaching CD's. Jeremy's ministry has been recognized by many national leaders and other prophetic leaders around the nation.

# Other Titles by Dr. Lopez

**Abandoned To Divine Destiny**: *You Were Before Time*

**Awakening to Prosperity**: *Setting Yourself Up to Live*

**Birthing Forth Your Prophetic Word**: *How to Make your Prophecy Come to Pass*

**Calling and Career**: *The Mystery of Discovering Divine Direction on Finding Success*

**Eye of the Seer**: *The School of the Seer, Dreams, Visions, Prophecy and More!*

**Releasing the Power of the Prophetic**: *A Practical Guide to Developing a Listening Ear and Discerning Spirit*

**School of the Prophets Advanced Training Manual**: *Diving into the Mystery of the Prophetic*

**School of the Prophets Manual**: *A Training Manual for Activating the Prophetic Spirit Within*

**The Laws of Financial Progression**: *Economic Principles for Success*

**The Power of the Eternal Now**: *Living in the Realm of I Am*

**The Power of Thought and Visualization:** *Thoughts become Things*

**The Seventh Day of the Lord**

**The Supply Dwells Within:** *The Treasure within Side of You*

**Wholeness:** *The Mystery of Healing in the Bible*

**You Were Born To Be an Entrepreneur:** *The Mystery of Discovering your Calling and Career*

Made in the USA  
Charleston, SC  
26 February 2015